A READING GUIDE TO

Roll of Thunder, Hear My Cry

by Mildred D. Taylor

D0048482

SCHOLASTIC

Scholastic BookFiles™

A READING GUIDE TO

Roll of Thunder, Hear My Cry

by Mildred D. Taylor

Laurie Rozakis, Ph.D.

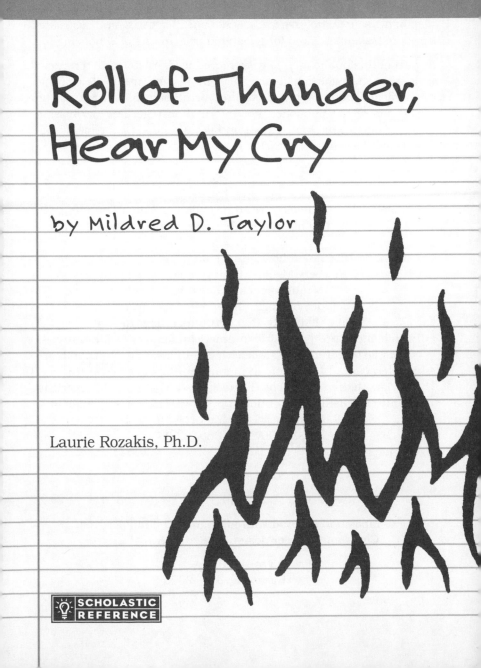

SCHOLASTIC
REFERENCE

Library of Congress Cataloging-in-Publication Data
Rozakis, Laurie.
Scholastic BookFiles: A Reading Guide to Roll of Thunder,
Hear My Cry by Mildred D. Taylor/Laurie Rozakis.
p. cm.
Summary: Discusses the writing, characters, plot, and themes
of this 1977 Newbery Medal–winning book. Includes discussion
questions and activities.
Includes bibliographical references (p.).
1. Taylor, Mildred D. Roll of thunder, hear my cry—
Juvenile literature.   2. African-American families in literature—
Juvenile literature.   3. Mississippi—In literature—Juvenile
lieterature.   4. Racism in literature—Juvenile literature.
[1. Taylor, Mildred D. Roll of Thunder, Hear My Cry.   2. American
literature—History and criticism.]   I. Title: A reading guide to
Roll of Thunder, Hear My Cry.   II. Title.
PS3570.A9463 R637 2003
813'.54–dc21   2002191232

0-439-46343-2

10 9 8 7 6 5 4 3 2 1   03 04 05 06 07

Composition by Brad Walrod/High Text Graphics, Inc.
Cover and interior design by Red Herring Design

Printed in the U.S.A.   23
First printing, July 2003

Contents

"By the time I entered high school,
I had a driving compulsion to paint
a truer picture of Black people....
I wanted to show a Black family
united in love and pride, of which the
reader would like to be a part."

—Mildred D. Taylor

Kids like you watch television, listen to CDs, and play video games for fun. Mildred D. Taylor's childhood was very different. She grew up enjoying her father's interesting stories about the Taylor family's life in the Mississippi countryside. Wilbert Lee Taylor, Mildred's father, sat by the fireplace in their home. There, he shared the family's past with Mildred, her older sister, Wilma, and their mother, Deletha. From these stories, Mildred Taylor learned that her family had courage, dignity, and self-respect.

Her father's magical storytelling ability made her want to share his talent. "I began to imagine myself as a storyteller, making people laugh at their own foibles [small faults] or nod their heads with pride about some stunning feat of heroism," she remembers.

The road to becoming an award-winning writer wasn't smooth and easy, however.

Mildred Taylor was born on September 13, 1943, in Jackson, Mississippi. Like the Logan family in *Roll of Thunder, Hear My Cry*, the Taylor family had lived in Mississippi since the days of slavery. That was very long ago, before 1865! However, when Mildred was just a tiny baby, her parents decided to make a new life in the North. The Taylors moved to Toledo, Ohio. They had a large family and many friends there. The family was close and loving.

The Taylors often took the long car trip back to Mississippi. They wanted to visit all their relatives. These trips were not happy all the time because black people and white people were kept apart in many parts of the South. This policy was called segregation. To segregate means to keep apart. Black people and white people could not use the same rest rooms, water fountains, or playgrounds. Blacks and whites had to eat in different parts of restaurants, too. Segregation made it very hard for black people to travel. It was hard on people's hearts and minds.

"Each trip down reminded us that the South into which we had been born . . . still remained," Taylor remembers. "On the rest rooms of gasoline stations were the signs WHITE ONLY, COLORED NOT ALLOWED. [In the past, black people were often called colored, which many people thought was insulting.] Over water fountains were the signs WHITE ONLY. In restaurant windows, in motel windows, there were always the signs WHITE ONLY, COLORED NOT ALLOWED. Every sign we saw proclaimed our second-class citizenship." These trips helped shape Taylor's goal to write about the proud African-American heritage she learned from her family. Her school experiences also helped her decide to become a writer.

When she was ten years old, Mildred Taylor was the only black child in her class. She was upset about the one-sided stories about black Americans in her history books. There was no pride in these stories. When she shared her own facts about black history with the class, however, everyone thought she was making things up. "I couldn't explain things to them," she said. "Even the teacher seemed not to believe me. They all believed what was in the history books," Taylor said. Since she was shy, Taylor did not say anything else. "So I turned to creating stories for myself, instead," she recalls.

In 1965, Taylor earned her college degree from the University of Toledo. From 1965 to 1967, she taught English and history to children in Africa. Then she studied at the University of Colorado's journalism school. Taylor worked hard to educate everyone in the university about the African-American experience. All the time, she kept thinking about making her family's stories her own.

In 1975, she wrote a story her father had told her about some trees that had been cut from the family's land in Mississippi. Taylor's story, "Song of the Trees," won first prize in the Council on Interracial Books for Children contest. A council is a group of people who work together on a project. This council's job was to bring people of different races together. They knew that Taylor's story could help black and white people understand one another.

Taylor expanded the story into a short novel, also called *Song of the Trees*. *The New York Times* newspaper named it an Outstanding Book of the Year in 1975. Taylor published *Roll of Thunder, Hear My Cry* in 1976. Her career as a writer had begun.

"It is my hope that to the children who read my books, the Logans will provide those heroes missing from the schoolbooks of my childhood, Black men, women, and children of whom they can be proud."

—Mildred D. Taylor

Sometimes, life isn't fair. We call this injustice. Racism is one of the worst injustices. Racism is judging people based on the color of their skin. Racist people think people of their color are better than people of another color. How can you deal with injustice and racism? Mildred Taylor found a way—through her writing. Taylor wrote *Roll of Thunder, Hear My Cry* to depict heroic African Americans. Taylor says, "I wanted to show a family united in love and self-respect, and parents, strong and sensitive, attempting to guide their children successfully, without harming their spirits, through the hazardous maze of living in a discriminatory [treating people unfairly] society."

Roll of Thunder, Hear My Cry takes place in 1933. Back then, black people and white people were separated by the Jim Crow laws. These laws enforced segregation. Segregation kept black people and white people apart. Black kids and white kids could not go to the same schools. People of different races couldn't travel in the same train cars, either. They *could* travel in the same buses, but black people had to sit in the back of the bus—until a white person got on. Then a black person had to give up his or her seat for the white person. Parks, cemeteries, and theaters were also marked WHITE or COLORED to prevent any contact between black and white people. The Jim Crow laws were meant to create "separate but equal" places for black and white people. It did not work out this way, however. The places were "separate," but they were not "equal."

For example, schools for black students got much less money than schools for white students. As a result, the schools for black students did not have enough textbooks, chalk, and other supplies. Many schools for black students did not have playing fields, school buses, or indoor bathrooms—but schools for white students often did.

Finally, in 1954, the Supreme Court got rid of the Jim Crow laws. The Supreme Court is the highest court in the United States. It has the power to change America's laws, but it doesn't have the power to change people's minds. Many people in the South were not willing to let black and white kids go to the same schools. The situation got so bad that in 1957, President Dwight D. Eisenhower had to send soldiers to Little Rock, Arkansas, to protect black kids going to a white school. The battle for equal rights continued.

In 1964, the Supreme Court passed the Civil Rights Act. This act made it against the law to discriminate against people because of their color. When you discriminate against someone, you do not treat them fairly. A year later, Congress passed the Voting Rights Act. This law made it easier for black people to vote. However, prejudice did not fade away at once. People were still "prejudging" others on the basis of their race. Mildred Taylor saw this herself.

Taylor went to school in Ohio. There were no Jim Crow laws there, so people of different races could learn, work, play, and travel side by side. However, when Taylor was a child in the 1950s, she took many trips to visit relatives in Mississippi. On these trips, she saw discrimination. In writing *Roll of Thunder, Hear My Cry,* Taylor used her own experiences with racism in the South to show what life may have been like for African Americans in the 1930s. She also tied in the stories her father had told about family members living under the Jim Crow laws during that time.

Taylor hopes that one day *Roll of Thunder, Hear My Cry* "will be instrumental in teaching children of all colors the tremendous influence Cassie's generation had in bringing about the civil rights movement of the fifties and sixties." She thanks her father for his help. She says, "Without his teachings, without his words, my words would not have been."

Chapter Charter:
Questions to Guide Your Reading

The following questions will help you think about the important parts of each chapter.

Chapter 1
- How are the African-American students treated? Do you think this is fair?
- What happened to the Berry family? What does this event tell you about racism in the South in the 1930s?
- Would you like to be friends with the Logan children? Why or why not?

Chapter 2
- Why has Mr. Morrison come to live with the Logans?
- What danger did the African-American people in the community face because of their color?
- What might it feel like to be the victim of hatred?

Chapter 3
- Why does the driver of the white children's school bus splash the Logan children with mud?
- How do the children get their revenge on the white bus driver and his passengers? Do you think this was right?
- What might it feel like to be the only person in town to have a big, fancy car?

Chapter 4

- What is your first clue that T.J. is big trouble? Do you think it's wise that Stacey is friends with him?
- How do you think Stacey felt when he had to tell his parents about his fight with T.J.?
- What does Cassie learn about her family from Big Ma?

Chapter 5

- Why does Big Ma park the wagon far away from the entrance to the market in Strawberry?
- Do you think Cassie should have demanded that Mr. Barnett wait on them at the store? Why or why not?
- How do you think Cassie felt at the end of her day in Strawberry?

Chapter 6

- Why does Big Ma try to stop Cassie from telling Uncle Hammer about their day in Strawberry?
- Mama tells Cassie, "Baby, we have no choice of what color we're born or who our parents are or whether we're rich or poor. What we do have is some choice over what we make of our lives once we're here." What do you think she means by this?
- Would you rather have Papa or Uncle Hammer as your father? Why?

Chapter 7

- How do you think Uncle Hammer felt when he saw T.J. wearing Stacey's new coat?

- Why does Mr. Jamison agree to put up the credit for the black families to shop in Vicksburg?
- How do you know that Mr. Morrison had a hard, painful life?

Chapter 8

- Papa tells Cassie, "There are things you can't back down on, things you gotta take a stand on. But it's up to you to decide what them things are." What things do you think Cassie must take a stand on? Why?
- Do you think it was a good decision for Cassie to take revenge on Lillian Jean? Is it okay to do mean things if you feel you have been treated unfairly?
- How do you think Mama felt when Kaleb Wallace fired her from her teaching job?

Chapter 9

- Would you spend time with the Simms boys? Why or why not?
- How was Papa injured? Why do you think this happened?
- What do you think will happen at the end of the book?

Chapter 10

- Why do you think the bank suddenly wants the Logans to pay their mortgage in full?
- Do you think the Logans' troubles with the Wallaces are over? Why or why not?
- What do you think will happen to T.J. in Strawberry?

Chapter 11

- How did T.J. get so badly injured?

- Would you have helped T.J. if you had been in Stacey's place? Why or why not?
- What do think will happen to the Avery family, especially T.J.?

Chapter 12

- What is your first clue that Papa set the fire?
- Papa says, "This thing's been coming a long time, baby...." What do you think he means by this?
- How can you tell that the Logans are a close and loving family?
- How would you feel if you were T.J.?

Plot: What's Happening?

"You ain't never had to live on nobody's place but your own and long as I live and the family survives, you'll never have to."

−Papa, *Roll of Thunder, Hear My Cry*

Roll *of Thunder, Hear My Cry* is the story of the Logan family, African-American farmers living in Mississippi in the 1930s. The Logans successfully battle racism to keep their land and stay together as a family.

When the story opens, nine-year-old Cassie Logan is walking to the first day of school. She's with her three brothers: Stacey (age twelve), Christopher-John (seven) and Clayton Chester (called "Little Man," six). The family owns four hundred acres of fine land. Half the land is mortgaged. This means the family had to borrow money from a bank to buy the land and now have to make a payment to the bank every month. Not until all the money is paid back, will the Logans own the land free and clear. Papa works on the railroad far away to pay the loan. Mr. Granger, a white man, wants to take the land from them. The land is very important to the Logans.

T.J. Avery, a thirteen-year-old troublemaker, tells how the Berrys, three black men, were burned—one killed—by the white Wallace brothers. A white boy, Jeremy Simms, joins the Logans as they walk to school. Jeremy goes to the white Jefferson Davis School while the Logan children attend the black Great Faith School.

Little Man and Cassie are so happy to get schoolbooks for the very first time! Their delight turns to rage when they get the tattered old books the white students had used for many years and thrown away. Cassie's mama is a seventh-grade teacher in the school. She understands how hurt her children feel, so she pastes paper over the inside covers of her students' books. These hide the pages that show that the white students had thrown the books away. Later, Papa returns unexpectedly from the railroad with Mr. Morrison, a big, strong man who lost his job. Mr. Morrison will be staying with the Logans. Papa tells the children to keep away from the Wallaces' store because people get in trouble there. Papa also knows the Wallaces have attacked other black families.

Little Man is upset because the white children have a school bus but the black students have to walk. After the school bus forces them into the mud, the Logan kids dig a deep trench. It fills with rainwater. When the bus falls into the trench, it is badly damaged.

Later, Mama takes the kids to visit the Berry family. Mr. Berry is burned very badly and cannot speak. "The Wallaces did that, children," Mama explains. "They poured kerosene over Mr. Berry and his nephews and lit them afire." To protest the attacks, Mama and Papa try to stop black people from shopping in the Wallace and Barnett stores.

T.J. and Stacey are in Mama's class. T.J. gets Stacey into trouble by giving him cheat notes. Mama disciplines Stacey. Later, Stacey beats up T.J. to get even with him. Stacey realizes that T.J. is not a good friend. He knows that T.J. is going down the wrong path in life.

Cassie is happy to visit the Saturday market in Strawberry. But the day turns out badly. Cassie gets angry at the store owner when he helps white people and lets the black people wait. Furious, the storeowner tells Cassie to get her "little black self" back to waiting. Then Cassie bumps into Lillian Jean, a white girl, and is forced to apologize.

The Logan children are thrilled when Uncle Hammer comes to visit for Christmas. Hammer drives the family around in his beautiful new car. Mr. Morrison tells the tragic story about his family getting killed by an angry white mob. A few days later, Mr. Granger threatens to take away the Logans' land if they don't make people start shopping in town again.

Cassie beats up Lillian Jean until she apologizes for what happened in Strawberry. Mama catches T.J. cheating and fails him on a test. T.J. tells everyone that Mama pasted over the pages in the schoolbooks. The school board fires Mama.

Papa, Mr. Morrison, and Stacey go shopping in Vicksburg. On the way home, someone shoots at Papa. The bullet skims his head! In the fight that follows, Papa's leg is broken. At the same time, the bank demands that the Logans' whole loan be paid all at once! Uncle Hammer sells his car to pay the debt.

During the night, T.J. comes running to the Logans. He explains that he broke into the mercantile store with the Avery brothers. The brothers beat up the store owners and T.J. The Logan children take T.J., who is badly hurt, home.

A white mob gathers at the Avery house. They want to hang T.J. Papa and Mr. Morrison run to the Avery home. Soon, Mama notices the cotton is on fire! Mama, Big Ma, and the mob go fight the fire. It starts to rain, which puts out the fire.

Everyone thinks lightning started the fire, but Cassie realizes that Papa set it to stop the hangings. T.J. will likely be put on the chain gang where he could die. Cassie cries.

Thinking about the plot
• Why is the land so important to the Logans?
• How do you know that the Logans stick together and help everyone?
• Which part of the story did you find the most exciting? Why?

"We walked in silence down the narrow cow path which wound through the old forest to the pond. As we neared the pond, the forest gapped open into a wide, brown glade."

—Cassie, *Roll of Thunder, Hear My Cry*

Roll of Thunder, Hear My Cry is set in a specific place—the Mississippi countryside—at a specific time—1933. The setting is so realistic that we almost feel like we're walking down the dusty roads with Cassie and her brothers, smelling the sweet pine trees and listening to the buzzing of lazy bees in the hot sunshine. Let's look at the novel's time and place one at a time.

Time: When does the story take place?

Roll of Thunder, Hear My Cry takes place in 1933. At that time, many people did not have the rights that we have today. Even if the rights were guaranteed by law, the law was not always obeyed. This was sometimes the case in the South, where many whites did not always want to give blacks the rights they were guaranteed.

The Civil War had ended a long time ago, in 1865. That year, the Thirteenth Amendment gave black Americans citizenship. Congress passed the Fifteenth Amendment five years later, in 1870. This amendment said that all American men had the right to vote, no matter their race or color. But as you have learned, racism did not go away quickly.

After the Civil War, parts of the South that were destroyed during the war began to be rebuilt. This period is known as Reconstruction. The government sent soldiers to the South to help make sure black people were treated fairly. Many southern white people resented the troops. In 1877, the government sent all the soldiers home, but there were still very hard feelings about rights for blacks. As you read, the Jim Crow laws (see page 9) restricted the rights of black people.

The differences in schooling available to black and white children show the inequality that ran through society even in the 1930s. In *Roll of Thunder, Hear My Cry*, Taylor describes how the black children walk for an hour or more to get to school, but the white students have buses. This shows that society considered the black students inferior to the white students. For example, the white students have a "long white wooden building" with a sports field and rows of benches. They have new schoolbooks, too.

The school for the black students, in contrast, is "four weather-beaten wooden houses on stilts of brick." There are only 7 teachers for 320 students. A cow is used to clip the wide crabgrass lawn, rather than having it cut. Since they are needed in the fields, the black students have a very short school year: It runs from October to March. Even so, many of the students can't start school until December, after the last wisp of cotton has been picked.

The white children's school is named for Jefferson Davis, the president of the Confederacy. The Confederacy was a group of eleven states that withdrew from the United States in 1860–1861. This led to the Civil War. In the novel, the Mississippi flag flies over the white children's school. The design of the Mississippi state flag contains the bars and stripes of the Confederate flag. At the white children's school, the flag of the United States flies below the Mississippi flag. According to tradition, the American flag should always be the top flag. By switching the order of the flags, Taylor shows that in the South in the 1930s, racism had won out over equality.

Nearly everyone in rural Mississippi in the 1930s was poor. Many of the people in the rest of America were poor, too, because on October 29, 1929, the stock market collapsed. The country plunged into the Great Depression. Taylor suggests the deep poverty by describing how T.J. and Claude cannot afford shoes. Mama has shoes, but she patches the holes in the soles with cardboard. By 1933, one quarter of all the workers in the country were unemployed—thirteen million people. In the novel, Mr. Morrison has lost his job on the railroad. Because there were so few jobs, people took any work available. Papa, for example, works most of the year away from his family on the railroad in Louisiana.

In *Roll of Thunder, Hear My Cry*, Mildred Taylor also tells about the "night men" who try to kill black people in many ways. They attacked some black people and covered others in tar and feathers. They also set some black people on fire, like the Berry men. The "night riders" hanged black people, too. These hangings were called lynchings. "Night riders" was another name for members of the Ku Klux Klan.

The Klan (as it is often called), a secret terrorist group, started right after the Civil War. Members of the Klan believed that white people were better than black people. Therefore, they resented the rise of former slaves to positions of equality to white people. Wearing white sheets and masks topped with pointy hoods, Klan members terrorized black people. They also attacked white people who tried to help black people, especially Catholics and Jews. Talking to Mama about the Wallaces terrorizing black people, Mr. Jamison, the lawyer, says, "You're not only accusing them of murder, which in this case would only be a minor consideration because the man killed was black, but you're saying they should be punished for it. That they should be punished just as if they had killed a white man, and punishment of a white man for a wrong done to a black man would denote equality. Now *that* is what Harlan Granger absolutely will not permit."

In 1924, about three million people claimed to belong to the Ku Klux Klan. During the 1930s, when *Roll of Thunder, Hear My Cry* takes place, the Klan was weaker but still had enough members to terrorize people across the South. Klan members were rarely stopped, as Mama says when she tells the children about the Wallaces burning the Berry men: "Everyone knows they did it, and the Wallaces even laugh about it, but nothing was ever done." Brave Mr. Jamison steps in to help members of the black community, but other people in the South in the 1930s believed that it was all right to attack blacks. Some were too terrified to stop the Klansmen.

As black people sought their civil rights in the 1950s, the Klan continued to strike. Klan members used bombs and other violent means to try to prevent black people from getting their rights. Because of First Amendment rights, which guarantee everyone's freedom of speech, the Klan still exists today although law enforcement officials closely monitor their activities.

Place: Where are we?

As a child, Mildred D. Taylor spent summers in Jackson, Mississippi, so she knows firsthand about the beautiful southern countryside. She knows about its soft beauty and its simple joys. She described her visits to Mississippi this way: "Running barefoot in the heat of the summer sun, my skin darkening to a soft, umber hue; chasing butterflies in the day, fireflies at night; riding an old mule named Jack and a beautiful mare named Lady; even picking a puff of cotton or two—there seemed no better world."

Taylor paints the beauty of Mississippi in *Roll of Thunder, Hear My Cry* by using vivid sensory details and descriptions. These are words that appeal to the five senses: sight, touch, smell, taste, and hearing.

Cassie loves going into the family's woods and fields. In March, Cassie says, "I was eager to be in the fields again, to feel the furrowed rows of damp, soft earth beneath my feet; eager to walk barefooted through the cool forest, hug the trees, and sit under their protective shadow."

It's not always nice weather in the Mississippi countryside, however. Taylor also helps the reader picture the scene by describing the heat, dust, and rain. "At the end of October the rain had come, falling heavily upon the six-inch layer of dust which had had its own way for more than two months," she writes. The rain turns the dust into "a fine red clay that oozed between our toes and slopped against our ankles as we marched miserably to and from school."

Taylor also helps readers imagine the setting by having her characters speak in the *dialect* of the Mississippi countryside. Dialect is the way people speak in a certain area. In a dialect, certain words are spelled and pronounced differently. For example, Little Man tells Cassie: "Y'all go ahead and get dirty if y'all wanna." "Y'all" is southern dialect for "You all." The dialect helps us hear how the characters sound so we can visualize how they look and act, too.

The characters also use the word "ain't," instead of "is not," "are not," or "am not." The characters might say, "He ain't going." This is part of the dialect. Long ago, the word "ain't" was accepted as a contraction for "am not." However, the word "ain't" should not be used today in everyday speech or formal writing. We would say, "He isn't going."

Thinking about the setting

- When and where does *Roll of Thunder, Hear My Cry* take place?
- How does Taylor use dialect to make the setting come alive?
- Do you think the events of this book could take place in a different setting? Why or why not?

"Then if you want something and it's a good thing and you got it in the right way, you better hang on to it and don't let nobody talk you out of it. You care what a lot of useless people say 'bout you and you'll never get anywhere, 'cause there's a lotta folks don't want you to make it."

—Uncle Hammer, *Roll of Thunder, Hear My Cry*

The theme of a literary work is its main idea. It's a general statement about life. *Roll of Thunder, Hear My Cry* has three main themes: the importance of family, the importance of owning land, and the importance of self-respect and the respect of others.

The importance of family

No one has to teach Cassie that family comes first: She knows it like she knows the fresh smell of the forest air or the soft touch of cotton. Nonetheless, the lesson is reinforced often. She learns how important family is from her papa, mama, and grandmother, Big Ma.

Papa tells Cassie that the family is like the fig tree that grows in the yard. The big oak and walnut trees almost overshadow the little fig. "But the fig tree's got roots that run deep," Papa says, "and it belongs in the yard as much as the oak and walnut. It keeps on blooming, bearing good fruit year after year, knowing all the time it'll never get as big as them other trees. Just keeps on growing and doing what it gotta do. It don't give up. It give up, it'll die. There's a lesson to be learned from that little tree, Cassie girl, 'cause we're like it. We keep doing what we gotta, and we don't give up. We can't." The family fights on to do what is right and to stay together.

At Christmas, Mr. Morrison tells the Logans how he lost his family to "night men," the Ku Klux Klan (see page 23). Mr. Morrison's mother thought first of saving her children—not herself. "She tried to get back into the house to save the girls, but she couldn't," Mr. Morrison explains. "Them night men was all over her and she threw me—just threw me like I was a ball—hard as she could, trying to get me away from them. Then she fought. Fought like a wild thing right 'side my daddy." This sad story shows us how Mr. Morrison's parents put their children first.

Mr. Morrison also puts family first. He risks his life by staying to protect the Logans against the Wallaces and others who hate people because of their skin color. He saves Papa's life when the Wallaces attack. He treats Stacey like a son. He teaches Stacey right from wrong when Stacey goes to the Wallace store and fights with T.J.

The importance of family is also shown in the Logans' support of one another. For example, when Mama is fired from her teaching job, Papa tells her that everything will be fine. The family depends on Mama's salary to survive, but still Papa comforts Mama. As he gently pushes a stray hair back over Mama's ear, he says, "We'll get by. . . . Plant more cotton maybe. But we'll get by." Papa's voice is quiet and calming.

Big Ma's stories show the importance of family, too. In Chapter 4, for instance, Big Ma tells Cassie how the family started. We can tell that Big Ma admires her late husband Paul Edward's courage, hard work, and talent as a carpenter.

Paul Edward had a good job, but he wanted to be a farmer on his own land. Paul Edward bought two hundred acres from a white man, Mr. Hollenbeck, and settled on the land with Big Ma. They had six children. Only Pa and Hammer lived.

When Paul Edward paid off the first two hundred acres in 1910, he wanted to buy more land. Then his children and their children would have their own land. They could be independent. In 1918, Mr. Jamison sold Paul Edward another two hundred acres. "I can see my Paul Edward's face the day Mr. Jamison sold him them two hundred acres," Big Ma recalls. "He put his arms 'round me and looked at his new piece of land, then he said 'zactly the same thing he said when he grabbed himself that first two hundred acres. Said, 'Pretty Caroline, how you like to work this fine piece of earth with me?' Sho' did . . . said the 'zact same thing."

Big Ma tells Cassie the story over and over so Cassie will remember it and tell it to her children. Cassie knows the story so well that she can tell it along with Big Ma. We know that Cassie will be able to pass on the stories of her family.

The importance of the land

"I asked him once why he had to go away, why the land was so important. He took my hand and said in his quiet way: 'Look out there, Cassie girl. All that belongs to you. You ain't never had to live on nobody's place but your own and as long as I live and the family survives, you'll never have to. That's important. You may not understand that now, but one day you will. Then you'll see.'"

–Cassie, *Roll of Thunder, Hear My Cry*

Family is the most important part of the Logans' life, but the land helps the family survive. Over and over, Big Ma, Mama, and Papa tell their children that the family will hold on to their land. Given the history of slavery in the southern states, owning land comes to stand for freedom for the Logans and many other families.

Because they own land, the Logans can grow and sell their own crops. They are not sharecroppers. They do not have to work on someone else's land as most of their friends and neighbors must do. They don't have to pay rent to a landowner for farming his land. As a result, they can keep most of the money they earn. The Logans have a mortgage on some of their land, but they have enough money so they don't need any other loans and other credit from the white landowners. As a result, they can shop wherever they want. Because the Logans own their own land, they have opportunities that other black families do not have.

Mr. Granger sees the land as a way to control black people and a way to make money. The Logans, in contrast, see the land as another way to be independent and keep the family together. Cassie recalls how Papa reached out and softly touched her face in the dark: "If you remember nothing else in your whole life, Cassie girl, remember this: We ain't never gonna lose this land. You believe that?" he says.

To help make sure the land stays in the family, Big Ma gives the land to her sons, Papa and Hammer. Cassie says that it doesn't matter which family members own the land because it will always be "Logan land."

Cassie loves the land. But no matter how much the family loves the land and the freedom it brings, people always come first.

Papa sets his cotton fields on fire to save T.J.'s life. This is Cassie's most important lesson. Cassie realizes this when she says: "Papa had found a way, as Mama had asked, to make Mr. Granger stop the hanging: He had started the fire."

When Cassie realizes the seriousness of the threats to her family and their land, she cries, "What had happened to T.J. in the night I did not understand but I knew that it would not pass. And I cried for those things which had happened in the night and would not pass. I cried for T.J. For T.J. and the land." Now that she is becoming more mature, Cassie is starting to understand the hard choices that adults must often make.

Self-respect and the respect of others

"You have to demand respect in this world, ain't nobody just gonna hand it to you. How you carry yourself, what you stand for—that's how you gain respect. But, little one, ain't nobody's respect worth more than your own. You understand that?"

– Papa, *Roll of Thunder, Hear My Cry*

The Logan family stays together through bad times. They hold on to their land when powerful people try to rip it away. Most of all, the Logans keep their pride and earn the respect of people who know them. Papa, Mama, and Big Ma teach their children the values that make their dignity and success possible.

Early on, Mama pastes over the hateful book pages that show the black students are getting the books the white students have thrown out. When Cassie's teacher tells Mama that she's spoiling the students, Mama says, "Maybe so, but that doesn't mean they have to accept them [the books] . . . and maybe we don't either." This shows us that Mama has self-respect and works to ensure her students' self-respect as well.

Mr. Morrison helps Stacey protect his pride when he lets Stacey tell his parents about the fight with T.J. in the Wallace store. When Stacey's eyes meet Mr. Morrison's eyes, we can see the respect between them. Cassie notices that "the two of them smiled in subtle understanding, the distance between them fading."

Cassie learns that racism is something to fight when possible, and something to put up with for safety's sake when necessary. She sees how wise her family is when they stop shopping at Mr. Wallace's store and help their neighbors fight injustice. She sees how smart her father is to set the fire in the cotton field to stop the mob from hanging T.J. Cassie learns the lesson about pride and respect Mama teaches her: "Everybody born on this earth is somebody and nobody, no matter what color, is better than anybody else."

Thinking about the themes

- Of the three themes, which do you think is the main one? Why?
- How important is land to you? Explain how you feel about the places where you have lived.
- What makes you feel good about yourself? How do you earn the respect of others?

"I loved to help Mama dress. She always smelled of sunshine and soap."

—Cassie, *Roll of Thunder, Hear My Cry*

R oll of Thunder, Hear My Cry focuses on Cassie Logan, the nine-year-old African-American girl who tells the story, and her family. Here's a brief overview of the characters.

The Logans (African-American landowning farmers)

Cassie Logan	the nine-year-old narrator
Stacey Logan	Cassie's twelve-year-old brother
Christopher-John	Cassie's seven-year-old brother
Little Man (Clayton Chester)	Cassie's six-year-old brother
Papa (David Logan)	Cassie's father
Mama (Mary Logan)	Cassie's mother
Uncle Hammer	Papa's brother
Big Ma (Caroline Logan)	Cassie's sixty-year-old grandmother
Mr. Morrison	the tall, big man who lives with the Logans; not a relative

The Averys (African-American sharecroppers)

T.J.	Stacey's thirteen-year-old friend
Claude	T.J.'s younger brother
Mr. Avery	T.J. and Claude's father
Mrs. Avery	T.J. and Claude's mother

The Simmses (white neighbors)

Jeremy Simms	an eleven-year-old white boy
Lillian Jean	Jeremy's twelve-year-old sister
Melvin	Jeremy's older brother
R.W.	Jeremy's older brother
Charlie Simms	the children's father

The Wallaces (white general-store owners)

Kaleb	store owner
Dewberry	Kaleb's son
Thurston	Kaleb's son

Other Characters

John Henry Berry	a sharecropper burned to death by white men
Samuel and Beacon Berry	sharecroppers badly burned by white men
Mr. Jamison	a lawyer
Harlan Granger	a plantation owner

Let's get to know the main characters a little better.

Cassie Logan: Nine-year-old Cassie is the novel's main character. She's smart, sassy, and self-confident. She's not afraid to speak her mind, too. Like her uncle Hammer, Cassie has a quick temper and strong sense of justice. We see this when Miss Crocker, Cassie's teacher, gives her students the tattered books the white students have thrown out. Cassie tells Miss Crocker how bad this makes her feel, even though she knows she can get whipped for talking back. Cassie says, "See, Miz Crocker, see what it says. They give us these ole books when they didn't want 'em no more." When Miss Crocker can't understand Cassie's pain, Cassie refuses to accept the textbook: "Miz Crocker," she says, "I don't want my book neither."

Cassie loves her parents, Uncle Hammer, and grandmother Big Ma. Like them all, Cassie is proud, hardworking, and deeply attached to the family's land. Unlike the adults in her family, however, Cassie doesn't understand the racial attitudes of her time and place. She doesn't understand that in Mississippi in the 1930s, African Americans did not have the same chances as whites.

The lessons about racial problems in the South come from many sources. Cassie's experiences with Lillian Jean Simms show her that white children her own age can judge people on their color. Cassie is shocked when Lillian Jean orders her off the sidewalk by saying, "You can't watch where you going, get in the road. Maybe that way you won't be bumping into decent white folks with your nasty self."

The owner of the mercantile store in Strawberry, Jim Lee Barnett, gives Cassie a cruel lesson in hate when he refuses to wait on her. Cassie sees real violence and injustice when her neighbors are burned to death and hanged. She also sees hate when she's told that T.J. could be sent to a chain gang. Cassie knows that if that happens, T.J. would be chained to other prisoners and forced to work along the roads and in the fields. Cassie learns that race does matter in Mississippi in the 1930s. She learns that the difference between black and white can sometimes be the difference between life and death.

Cassie grows up during the year described in the book. As Mama tells Cassie after she runs into hatred in Strawberry: "Baby, you had to grow up a little today. I wish . . . well, no matter what I wish. It happened and you have to accept the fact that in the world outside this house, things are not always as we would have them be." As she learns the sad truths about her world, Cassie also comes to cherish her family's deep strength, unity, and love.

Stacey Logan: Cassie's twelve-year-old brother is the oldest Logan child. Stacey likes to boss his brothers and sister around. They look up to him because he is a leader. Also, his parents trust and respect him. Stacey comes up with many of their most dangerous projects, like creating the huge ditch that wrecks the school bus. Stacey also disobeys his parents' order to stay away from the Wallace store when he chases T.J. there and beats him up. Stacey is rebellious enough to disobey his parents. However, he is not mature enough to fully understand the bad things that can happen if he does not obey.

Stacey is also proud, loyal, and honest. Stacey refuses to cheat with T.J. on the test. After Mama catches T.J. cheating, Stacey doesn't turn T.J. in, even though it means that he gets a public whipping from his mother.

Like Cassie, Stacey grows up during the year described in the book. Stacey becomes aware of the hatred that blacks faced in the South in the 1930s. This leads him to make tough choices. For example, he pushes away his white friend Jeremy because it can be dangerous for blacks to be friends with whites. Stacey also ends his friendship with T.J. because T.J. gets into too much trouble. However, in the end, Stacey proves his maturity, bravery, and loyalty by helping T.J. Cassie thinks, "As far back as I could remember, Stacey had felt a responsibility for T.J. I had never really understood why. Perhaps he felt that even a person as despicable as T.J. needed someone he could call 'friend,' or perhaps he sensed T.J.'s vulnerability better than T.J. did himself."

Papa (David Logan): Cassie's father is hardworking, brave, and wise. To earn the money the family needs to keep their land, Papa works for much of the year on the railroad. Papa's wisdom and caring are shown when he brings Mr. Morrison to live with the Logans.

Papa also stands up for himself and his family. His actions show his bravery and self-respect. For example, Papa risks his life to stop people from shopping at the Wallace store. He does this because Mr. Wallace burned a black man to death. The Wallaces shoot at Papa's head and his leg is broken in the fight, but he does not stop fighting hatred.

We see Papa's values most of all at the end of the book. Papa is willing to use his shotgun to protect T.J. but instead uses his brains: He sets the cotton fields on fire. Everyone runs to fight the fire. This stops the men who want to hang T.J. Papa burns his crops even though he loses a quarter of his cotton. This shows that Papa values family and friends more than money.

Mama (Mary Logan): Cassie's mother is a teacher. She loves her job and is very good at it. "She's born to teaching like the sun is born to shine," Papa says with love. Mama is proud of being black and very aware of hatred against black people. To help her students' self-esteem, she covers the pages of the textbooks that show the white students threw out the books the black students are now using. Mama also fights racism by teaching her students about the evils of slavery. Mama's bravery gets her fired from her teaching job.

Mama is wise. She tells Cassie, "Baby, we have no choice of what color we're born or who our parents are or whether we're rich or poor. What we do have is some choice over what we make of our lives once we're here." Mama looks deep into Cassie's eyes and says, "And I pray to God you'll make the best of yours."

Mama doesn't complain when the family runs low on money. She does the best she can to keep the family running smoothly. For this, her husband and children love and respect her very much.

Uncle Hammer (Papa's brother): Like Cassie, Hammer has a quick temper and is not willing to accept hatred against black people. He moved to Chicago to have more chances to be successful and to get ahead. When he comes back home to Mississippi, he gets angry about the racism. "A black man's life ain't worth the life of a cowfly down here," he says bitterly. Hammer tries to attack Charlie Simms for the bad way he treated Cassie. Mr. Morrison stops Hammer before he hurts Charlie Simms or himself.

Hammer is very generous and loyal to his family. He visits his family every Christmas and brings fine gifts. Like the rest of his family, Hammer thinks the Logans' land is very important. We see this when he sells his fancy car to pay the loan on the land. The children know he is a fine man, and they love him very much.

Big Ma (Caroline Logan): Papa's mother, Big Ma, runs the Logan farm. Wise, kind, and loving, Big Ma passes on the family stories to Cassie. We see that Big Ma is smart when she gives the land to her sons. This protects the land from Harlan Granger, who wants to take it from them. Big Ma is good at helping sick people, too. She helps many people, especially those hurt by white violence, including the Berrys. She is very religious.

Mr. Morrison: He is a very tall and strong black man who comes to live with the Logans when he loses his job. Mr. Morrison helps farm the Logan land and becomes an important part of their family. Since he is so strong, Mr. Morrison helps protect the Logans while Papa is away working on the railroad. He also helps the children think about what is right and wrong His family was killed by members of the Ku Klux Klan when he was just six years old.

T.J. Avery: T.J. gets into a lot of trouble. He fails the seventh grade, cheats on tests, gets Mama fired, and hangs out at the Wallace store. His poor choices lead Stacey to break off their friendship. T.J. shows bad judgment many times, especially when he teams up with the older, white Simms brothers. T.J. is with the Simms brothers when he steals a gun from the store. Then, he is in the room when the Simms brothers beat the store owners. As a result, T.J. is nearly hanged. At the end of the book, he is sent to jail. Mr. Logan thinks T.J. might even be put on a chain gang and forced to work hard in the fields. A judge will decide T.J.'s punishment.

Thinking about the characters

- Would you like to be friends with Cassie? Why or why not?
- How does Cassie change during the novel?
- Which character in *Roll of Thunder, Hear My Cry* do you admire the most? Why?
- Why do you think T.J. gets into so much trouble? What help could you give him?

What have other people thought of *Roll of Thunder, Hear My Cry?* They think it's great! "The events and settings of the powerful novel are presented with such verisimilitude [like real life] and the characters are so carefully drawn that one might assume the book is autobiographical [about the author's life], if the author were not so young," said one adult reviewer. "This is a tremendously powerful, dramatic, and beautifully written book," wrote another critic in a major newspaper.

The person reviewing *Roll of Thunder, Hear My Cry* for *The New York Times Book Review* understood that the book describes indignities, insults to black people. This writer was impressed that Mildred Taylor wasn't nasty about the hatred her black characters had experienced. According to this critic, "Taylor... writes not with rancor [hatefulness] or bitterness of indignities, but with pride, strength, and respect for humanity."

Many critics admire how Taylor created the Logan family. The critics liked the love that Taylor had for Cassie, her brothers, and their parents. For example, a critic for the *Kirkus Reviews* wrote: "The strong, clearheaded Logan family ... are drawn with quiet affection."

What about the kids who read this book? Here's a review written by a child and posted on Amazon.com: "THIS IS THE GREATEST

BOOK I EVER READ!!!!!! I would recommend this to anyone with good taste because it has a lot of detail and meaning. I give it a 5 [out of 5] because of the great story line."

Adults and kids agree: *Roll of Thunder, Hear My Cry* is a great book. It's not surprising, then, that the novel has won many very impressive awards. These awards include being named a *New York Times Book Review* Best of Children's Books award, 1970–1980, and an American Library Association Notable Book. These are big awards given to books that tell important stories in a way that people enjoy. *Roll of Thunder, Hear My Cry* received an honor book citation from *The Boston Globe* and a Jane Addams Honor citation, too. The novel also won the Pacific Northwest Young Readers Award and was a finalist for a National Book Award. And there's more!

Look at the front cover of *Roll of Thunder, Hear My Cry.* Do you see the gold seal? That's proof of another important award: the Newbery Award. This prize is given every year to the writer who has made "the most distinguished contribution to American literature for children." *Roll of Thunder, Hear My Cry* became an instant classic when it won this award.

The book was published more than twenty-five years ago and is still very popular. As proof of its popularity and wide appeal, in 1978 the book was made into a miniseries for ABC-TV. Many people tuned in to the show. They enjoyed watching this story of the Logan family.

Thinking about what other people think of *Roll of Thunder, Hear My Cry*

• Which parts of this book seem most like real life? Which parts seem made up? Explain.

• One critic called *Roll of Thunder, Hear My Cry* "tremendously powerful, [and] dramatic." What do you think makes this book powerful and dramatic?

• Imagine that you were on the committee that awarded *Roll of Thunder, Hear My Cry* the Newbery Award. Why would you have voted to honor this book?

Glossary

Here are some important words and terms from *Roll of Thunder, Hear My Cry.* Understanding these words will make it easier for you to read the novel.

acre a unit of land measurement. One acre is equal to 43,560 square feet. The Logans own four hundred acres of land.

aloof distant; remote; detached from other people

bootleg Originally used to refer to alcohol made and sold illegally, the word is now often used to refer to any goods that are made and sold illegally. The word *bootleg* comes from the way people smuggled liquor by hiding the bottles in their tall boots.

boycott to avoid doing business with a person or a company to force them to take a specific action. The Logans and some of their neighbors boycott the Wallace store to protest the Wallaces' racism.

chain gang a form of punishment in which prisoners are chained together, especially when working outside

Confederacy the group of eleven Southern states that seceded from the United States in 1860–1861. When spelled with a lowercase *c, confederacy* means a group of people joined together to achieve a specific purpose.

Depression the Great Depression; the economic crisis that began with the stock market crash in 1929 and continued through the 1930s

fretting worrying

lynching a murder by a mob, usually by hanging

meticulously doing something carefully; playing close attention to detail

moping brooding or worrying.

mortgage the loan a bank gives to people so they can buy a house and/or land

nightriders a group of men, also called night men, who commit violent actions to scare people. The term is often used to refer to members of the Ku Klux Klan, a secret group of white men who suppressed the rights of African Americans and others.

Packard a type of automobile

plantation a farm or estate on which cotton, tobacco, or similar crops are grown. Plantations are located in warm climates, like the American South.

racism prejudice; the belief that one race of people is better than another race of people

ransack to search and mess everything up; to plunder

revenge to get back at someone for a hurt he or she has done to you

rural of or relating to country or agriculture

sharecroppers farmers who work someone else's land. They give the owner part of their crop as rent for the use of the land.

tenant farmer a sharecropper

testily in an irritable or cranky mood

triumphant successful; winning

uppity acting in an arrogant way; not knowing your supposedly appropriate place in society; often used in a derogatory way to describe African Americans who demanded equality.

wheedle to coax or beg

"I do not know how old I was when the daydreams became more than that, and I decided to write them down, but by the time I entered high school, I was confident that I would one day be a writer."

—Mildred D. Taylor

Even as a child, Mildred D. Taylor was determined to become a writer. She wanted to tell the stories of her childhood as they really happened, the stories her father had shared with her and her sister. But just wanting to be a writer isn't enough: It takes hard work and practice. Mildred Taylor knew this. To make her goal even more difficult, Taylor did not write easily or quickly. "I had never particularly liked to write, nor was I exceptionally good at it," she said in an interview. "But I had always been taught that I could achieve anything I set my mind to do," she added.

So Taylor struggled to get her ideas on paper and remain true to the pride she felt for her family and heritage. She did not fool herself that it would be easy. "Many times what I considered my best work was not good enough," she recalled. All during elementary school, junior high, and high school she kept at it. One day in high school she had a breakthrough when she wrote a story about her family. She used the first-person point of view. In a first-person story, the narrator, who is one of the characters, explains the events of the story through his or her own eyes, using the pronouns *I* and *me*. "Without realizing it," Taylor commented later, "I was telling the story in much the same language as when it was told to me. I was using the language of the family storytellers."

Reread some of *Roll of Thunder, Hear My Cry*. You will notice how the story is told in the first person, through Cassie's eyes. For example, Cassie says, "At the end of the examination day, I shot out of Miss Crocker's class and hurried into the yard. I was eager to get to the crossroads to meet Lillian Jean; I had promised myself to first take care of the examinations and then..." We see only what Cassie wants us to see. For example, we don't yet know what Cassie is going to do after the examinations because she doesn't tell us.

Finding her own voice and style

Taylor had yet to realize how important the breakthrough of using the first-person perspective was to her career. It took a long time for Taylor to understand that she had to use the language of the storytellers when she wrote. She was still struggling to find her *voice*, her own special way of writing. "Having read only fiction by white writers," she said, "I wanted to write like them, like the great writers we had studied in class—[Ernest] Hemingway, [Charles] Dickens, [Jane] Austen, and the like."

It took years for Taylor to unlock her unique voice and style. It happened almost by chance! One day, Taylor decided to enter a contest given by the Council on Interracial Books for Children. It was close to the deadline: She had only a few days before her entry was due. Since she didn't have time to write something new, Taylor looked through the stories she had already written to find one that might fit. She pulled out a story based on a tale her father had told her. Originally, Taylor had written the story from a boy's point of view, but the story was dull and artificial. Then she tried writing the story from the grandmother's point of view, but that was flat and unconvincing, too. Then Taylor rewrote the story in the first person through Cassie's eyes. Everything came together! "I'm not sure where she came from," Taylor said, "but suddenly she was there: Cassie Logan, the storyteller. . . . The storytelling tradition had always been in the first person. It was my heritage and I went with it." All weekend long, Taylor rewrote the story. She sent it in and waited.

A few months later, Taylor found out that she had won the contest! The story was published as "Song of the Trees." Taylor had discovered her voice and style.

Attention, all writers!

Taylor's struggle to become a writer shows the importance of searching for your own style and voice. Her hard work and determination prove the importance of the old saying, "Be true to yourself."

- **In literature as in life:** *Roll of Thunder, Hear My Cry* is based on a real-life story that Taylor heard from her father. Think of a real-life story from your family. It might be a story that an older relative told you or an event that you experienced yourself. Create a narrator, someone like Cassie Logan. Then, tell the story from the first-person point of view, as Taylor did. Use the pronouns *I* and *me.* Since you are writing fiction, you can change the facts to make the story more logical, funny, or emotional, for example. Share your story by reading it to your family or e-mailing it to a friend.

- **Fire!:** After the fire is out, Cassie looks at the fields. "Near the slope where once cotton stalks had stood, their brown bolls popping with tiny puffs of cotton, the land was charred, desolate, black, still steaming from the night." The fire is a terrible event, indeed. Write an article for the local newspaper about the big fire. Explain how it started, how it ended, and how much of Papa's crops were destroyed.

- **My special place:** Cassie likes to spend time in her family's woods. What special place do you like? Describe a place that's important to you. It might be your room, the seashore, or the park, for example. Using details that appeal to all five senses, just like Taylor does, describe how the place looks, smells, and sounds. Tell about the way things in the place feel, too.

• **Tell it in poetry:** Mildred Taylor chose to tell the story of Cassie and her family as a novel. How would the story have changed if it had been told as a poem? Retell *Roll of Thunder, Hear My Cry* as a ballad. A ballad is a story told in song form. Ballads have a strong rhythmic beat, like songs. If you want, include a refrain (a repeated word or phrase). Refrains are usually placed after groups of four or six lines. When you have finished your ballad, recite it to your classmates or family.

• **All's well that ends well?:** At the end of the novel, Cassie cries "for T.J. and the land." What does this mean? Does *Roll of Thunder, Hear My Cry* have a happy ending or a sad one? Rewrite the novel's ending to make it clearly happy or sad. Make sure that your ending makes sense with the events in the book. You can share your ending by reading it to a small group of classmates.

- **Origin of the title:** The book's title comes from a traditional slave song, called a spiritual. The words are

> *Roll of thunder*
> *hear my cry*
> *Over the water*
> *bye and bye*
> *Ole man comin'*
> *down the line*
> *Whip in hand to*
> *beat me down*
> *But I ain't*
> *gonna let him*
> *Turn me 'round*

Explain how this song fits the book's meaning. Then, share a song that has special meaning to you and your family. You can sing or play the song for a small group of classmates.

- **I'm like a . . . :** Papa tells Cassie that the family is like the fig tree that grows in the yard. Papa explains the lesson of the little tree: "We keep doing what we gotta, and we don't give up. We can't." Choose two objects from nature such as a plant, bird, place, or weather condition. Then, explain how they stand for one or more of your character traits. Draw a picture of the object that best shows your character.

- **Be a secret pal:** For Christmas, Jeremy Simms makes a wooden flute for Stacey. The flute has a sweet sound. There's something very special about a handmade gift like Jeremy's flute. Make a gift for your special friend.

First, think about someone you know who would like to get a handmade gift. The person might be a grandparent, a parent, a brother, a sister, or a neighbor. Then, decide when to give the gift to your "secret pal." You might give the gift for a special occasion such as a birthday, anniversary, or graduation. Or you might want to give the gift just to make someone smile!

Now, match the gift to the person and your abilities. Make something you do well that the person will really enjoy. Here are some ideas:

a scrapbook	a beaded friendship pin
a poem or a letter	an object from clay
a coupon book for chores	a baked good like a cake or a pie
a flower arrangement	a series of lessons
a craft	

- **Listen to the past:** In the Author's Note at the beginning of *Roll of Thunder, Hear My Cry*, Mildred Taylor explains that her father was a good storyteller.

Everybody has a story to tell. The story might be about the past, the person's family, or life in general. When you listen to someone tell about his or her life, you are helping to create an *oral history*. The history may never be written down, but it can be passed from person to person through the generations. This is what happened in Taylor's family and in Cassie's family.

Ask an older relative, friend, or neighbor to share an oral history of his or her life. Before the interview, list the questions you want to ask. You might like to write down the answers or you might use a video camera or an audiotape recorder. Be sure to ask your storyteller's permission before you begin. Here are some questions you might use:

- Tell me about your family. What games did you play with your family and friends?
- What foods did you eat when you were a child?
- What toys did you have?
- What was your school like? What subjects did you study? What books did you read?

After the interview, send a thank-you letter. You might want to give the person a copy of the tape or video, too.

- **Bake a batch of biscuits:** Cassie and her mother make biscuits together. Everyone likes biscuits because they are easy to make and taste great. There are many different ways to make biscuits. Here's a recipe that is sure to please everyone in your home. Make them with a parent, older brother or sister, or older friend.

Biscuit Ingredients

1¾ cup all-purpose flour + about ¼ cup extra

1 teaspoon salt

2½ teaspoons baking powder (not baking *soda!*)

4 tablespoons butter, margarine, or solid white shortening

⅔–¾ cup of milk

1. Ask for an adult's help and preheat oven to 450°.

2. Wash your hands.

3. In a big bowl, mix 1¾ cup flour, salt, and baking powder.

4. With a fork, mix in the butter, margarine, or shortening.

5. Mix in enough milk so that the dough leaves the sides of the bowl. This should take about 1 minute. (Overmixed biscuits get tough and chewy rather that soft and flaky.)

6. Sprinkle a little flour on a table or wooden board. Roll out the dough, and cut the biscuits with a biscuit cutter. (If you don't have a biscuit cutter, a plastic cup works great.)

7. Place the biscuits on a cookie sheet or other flat pan. Ask an adult to help you put the pan in the oven. Bake the biscuits until they are lightly browned, about 12 to 15 minutes. Eat with butter, jam, or whatever you like!

• **Forest fun:** Cassie likes to walk through the family's woods. From her explorations, Cassie has learned a lot about nature, too. Make a forest rubbing to learn about nature without disturbing it. Choose some tree bark, leaves, pine needles, or large rocks. You will need crayons and white paper. Then, follow these steps:

- Lay your paper against the thing from which you want a rubbing.
- Rub the crayon back and forth until the pattern shows. Be gentle!

Share your rubbings with a friend. See if your friend can guess whether your rubbings are bark, leaves, needles, or rocks. Collect a lot of different rubbings, and label them, too.

- **The perfect gift:** On Christmas morning, the children get wonderful gifts: books! There are two versions of *Aesop's Fables* for the two younger boys, *The Count of Monte Cristo* for Stacey, and *The Three Musketeers* for Cassie. Read one of these books, and explain why it would make a great gift for the character to whom it was given.

- **Goal-setter:** Mama and Cassie talk about Cassie's future. Mama tells Cassie, "We have some choice over what we make of our lives once we're here." Mama hopes that Cassie will make the right choices and have a happy and fulfilling life. What do you want to be when you grow up? Where would you like to live? How do you want to change the world? Talk with a parent or a teacher about your goals. Discuss what you can do now and in the future to make your goals come true.

- **Scrapbook:** Cassie treasures the land, but she also values other parts of her life. She likes spending time with her family, reading books, and being with her friends. *Roll of Thunder, Hear My Cry* helps Mildred Taylor remember important events in her family's life. Make a scrapbook about your life. Choose at least ten special times. These might be the arrival of a new family member, moving to a new home, or a family vacation, for example. Include photographs, drawings, and souvenirs from each event. Glue one souvenir on a page. Then write a caption or paragraph explaining its importance. Be sure to include the date and a brief description of the occasion, too!

Books about the Logan family and their friends by Mildred D. Taylor

These books are listed in the order in which the events unfold for the Logan family.

The Land, a prequel to *Roll of Thunder, Hear My Cry* (2001)
Roll of Thunder, Hear My Cry (1976)
Let the Circle Be Unbroken (1981)
Mississippi Bridge (1990)
The Road to Memphis (1990)
Song of the Trees (1975)
The Well: David's Story (1995)

Other books by Mildred D. Taylor

The Friendship (1987)
The Gold Cadillac (1987)

Civil rights books—nonfiction

The Civil Rights Movement for Kids: A History with 21 Activities by Mary Turck
The Day Martin Luther King, Jr., Was Shot by James Haskins
Frederick Douglass: The Last Day of Slavery by William Miller
If You Lived at the Time of Martin Luther King by Ellen Levine

I Have a Dream by Martin Luther King Jr., forward by Coretta Scott King

Martin's Big Words: The Life of Dr. Martin Luther King, Jr. by Doreen Rappaport

Oh, Freedom: Kids Talk About the Civil Rights Movement with the People Who Made It Happen by Casey King

Rosa Parks: From the Back of the Bus to the Front of a Movement by Camilla Wilson

Sojourner Truth: Ain't I a Woman by Patricia and Fredrick McKissak

Civil rights books—fiction

Belle Teal by Ann M. Martin

Beyond Mayfield by Vanda Nelson

Bud, Not Buddy by Christopher Paul Curtis

Freedom Songs by Yvette Moore

Heaven by Angela Johnson

The Skin I'm In by Sharon G. Flake

Sweet Clara and the Freedom Quilt by Deborah Hopkinson

The Watsons Go to Birmingham—1963 by Christopher Paul Curtis

Audiocassettes

Roll of Thunder, Hear My Cry is available on Bantam Books-Audio, read by Lynne Thigpen

Bibliography

Books

Children's Literature Review. Volume 9. Gale, 1985.

Contemporary Literary Criticism. Volume 21. Gale, 1982.

Dictionary of Literary Biography. Volume 52, *American Writers for Children Since 1960.* Gale, 1986.

Kovacs, Deborah and James Preller. *Meet the Authors and Illustrators.* New York: Scholastic, 1991.

Rees, David. *The Marble on the Water: Essays on Contemporary Writers of Fiction for Children and Young Adults.* Horn Book, 1980.

Something About the Author Autobiography Series. Volume 5. Gale, 1988.

Newspapers and magazines

Christian Science Monitor, November 3, 1976, p. 20; October 14, 1981, p. B1; October 5, 1984, p. B6.

Horn Book, August 1975, p. 384; December 1976, p. 627; August 1977, pp. 410–414; March/April 1989, pp. 179–182.

Los Angeles Times Book Review, January 3, 1988, p. 5.

The New York Times, February 3, 1982, p. 18.

The New York Times Book Review, May 4, 1975, p. 39; November 21, 1976, p. 62; November 15, 1981, p. 55; December 11, 1983, p. 43; November 15, 1987, p. 37; February 21, 1988, p. 33.

Publishers Weekly, October 22, 2001, p. 24.

School Librarian, March 1978, pp. 46–47.

Times Educational Supplement, November 18, 1977, p. 33.

Washington Post Book World, February 13, 1977, p. G10; April 23, 1978, p. E2; May 10, 1987, p. X15.

Web sites

Contemporary Authors Online, Gale, 2002. Reproduced in Biography Resource Center. Farmington Hills, Michigan.: The Gale Group, 2002.

http://www.galenet.com/servlet/BioRC

Teachers@Random:

www.randomhouse.com/teachers/authors/tayl./html

Educational Paperback Association:

http://www.edupaperback.org/authorbios/Taylor_Mildred

Mildred Taylor Teacher Resource File:

http://falcon.jmu.edu/~ramseyil/taylor.htm